The Spirit-Filled Woman

Harrison House
Tulsa, Oklahoma

The Spirit-Filled Woman
ISBN 0-89274-790-0
Copyright © 1996 by Harrison House
P.O. Box 35035
Tulsa, Oklahoma 74153

Introduction

The Spirit-Filled Woman is a powerful collection of quotations by women of our day used mightily by God. Prompted by the Spirit and supported by Scripture, this book is filled with insights for victorious, Spirit-filled living for you and your family.

The Spirit-Filled Woman is a treasure of strength and truth for daily living. Fill your life with these words of wisdom and renew your mind with the light of God's Word.

*G*od loves women! We are His unique creation! Each woman is created to be special. He is as concerned about you as He is about any other woman — or man.

Nancy Cole

My frame was not hidden from you when I was made in the secret place. When I was woven together in the depths of the earth, your eyes saw my unformed body. All the days ordained for me were written in your book before one of them came to be.

Psalm 139:15,16 NIV

*G*od sees every creation as good and perfect — and that's how you're to see yourself! When you see yourself that way, you will see your mate that way.

Pat Harrison

So God created man in his own image, in the image of God he created him; male and female he created them.

Genesis 1:27 NIV

*G*od's design for our lives is a perfect one, and the closer we can pattern our lives after His design, the happier we will be.

Margaret Hicks

And he said to them all, If any man will come after me, let him deny himself, and take up his cross daily, and follow me. For whosoever will save his life shall lose it: but whosoever will lose his life for my sake, the same shall save it.

Luke 9:23,24

*B*eing a woman of God is all about entrusting ourselves into God's care, regardless of what happens to us in life, and knowing that He cares for us and will provide for us.

Beverly LaHaye

Casting all your care upon him; for he careth for you.
1 Peter 5:7

We must be women of vision, confirming our confidence and assurance in our family by speaking God's Holy Word as final, undisputable authority against the delusions of the enemy.

Jeri Williams

Let us hold fast the profession of our faith without wavering; for he is faithful that promised.
Hebrews 10:23

You will be rewarded if you will make the commitment of standing true to God even in the hard places in life.

Oretha Hagin

Thou therefore endure hardness, as a good soldier of Jesus Christ. No man that warreth entangleth himself with the affairs of this life; that he may please him who hath chosen him to be a soldier.

2 Timothy 2:3,4

*W*hen you are in trouble, go to the throne before you go to the phone.

Joyce Meyer

Let us therefore come boldly unto the throne of grace, that we may obtain mercy, and find grace to help in time of need.

Hebrews 4:16

*H*appiness and inner peace come only through Christ Jesus. In order to have a character change, we must have a right relationship with God. Having that relationship we can learn to accept ourselves and others, just as we are, faults and all. That is a big accomplishment. This does not mean that we will not seek improvement or expect others to improve.

Bea Basansky

Therefore if any man be in Christ, he is a new creature: old things are passed away; behold, all things are become new. And all things are of God, who hath reconciled us to himself by Jesus Christ, and hath given to us the ministry of reconciliation.

2 Corinthians 5:17,18

*Y*ou were conceived and born with every ability, every talent, every beautiful ingredient you will ever need in all of your life. Tap into your God-created uniqueness through the adventure of the Jesus-life. God's ultimate dream for you is that you enjoy a golden lifestyle of happiness, success, health, prosperity and plenty!

Daisy Osborn

According as his divine power hath given unto us all things that pertain unto life and godliness, through the knowledge of him that hath called us to glory and virtue: Whereby are given unto us exceeding great and precious promises: that by these ye might be partakers of the divine nature, having escaped the corruption that is in the world through lust.

2 Peter 1:3,4

There is a great deal of power in a Holy Spirit-filled woman — power to turn every situation around for good!

Bea Basansky

But ye shall receive power, after that the Holy Ghost is come upon you: and ye shall be witnesses unto me both in Jerusalem, and in all Judaea, and in Samaria, and unto the uttermost part of the earth.

Acts 1:8

It is the power of the Holy Spirit working through the Word that brings victory to our lives.

Joyce Meyer

Through mighty signs and wonders, by the power of the Spirit of God; so that from Jerusalem, and round about unto Illyricum, I have fully preached the gospel of Christ.

Romans 15:19

When you pray, you get into the stream of (God's) power. All you have to do is yield yourself to God . . . and you'll soon find yourself being lifted above all obstacles, all storms, all difficulties.

Kathryn Kuhlman

And at midnight Paul and Silas prayed, and sang praises unto God: and the prisoners heard them. And suddenly there was a great earthquake, so that the foundations of the prison were shaken: and immediately all the doors were opened, and every one's bands were loosed.

Acts 16:25,26

*O*h, the sweetness of His presence when we pour our heart feelings out to Him, cry and laugh and listen to Him speak to our hearts those words of comfort and encouragement. Your time with God is your source of strength in life.

Sharon Daugherty

As the deer pants for streams of water, so my soul pants for you, O God. My soul thirsts for God, for the living God. When can I go and meet with God?
Psalm 42:1,2 NIV

17

We are created by God to be happy and to feel good about ourselves.

Joyce Meyer

Thou wilt shew me the path of life: in thy presence is fulness of joy; at thy right hand there are pleasures for evermore.

Psalm 16:11

Our self-worth and self-confidence as Christian women can be found in no other source than God's Word.

Jeri Williams

But he answered and said, It is written, Man shall not live by bread alone, but by every word that proceedeth out of the mouth of God.

Matthew 4:4

*Y*ou shall be blessed because you obey the voice of God.

Carolyn Savelle

Behold, I set before you this day a blessing and a curse; A blessing, if ye obey the commandments of the Lord your God, which I command you this day.

Deuteronomy 11:26,27

*D*are to dream . . . then turn your dreams into reality!

Cheryl Salem

I have strength for all things in Christ Who empowers me (I am ready for anything and equal to anything through Him Who infuses inner strength into me: I am self-sufficient in Christ's sufficiency).

Philippians 4:13 AMP

*I*t's not what happens to you; it's what you do with that thing after it happens.

Kathryn Kuhlman

But the God of all grace, who hath called us unto his eternal glory by Christ Jesus, after that ye have suffered a while, make you perfect, stablish, strengthen, settle you.
1 Peter 5:10

*J*t is essential to free your heart of anger and bitterness toward God and anyone else so that your prayers will not be hindered.

Dodie Osteen

Therefore I say unto you, What things soever ye desire, when ye pray, believe that ye receive them, and ye shall have them. And when ye stand praying, forgive, if ye have ought against any: that your Father also which is in heaven may forgive you your trespasses.

Mark 11:24,25

*I*t's important to set priorities in your life. Establish what things are of most importance, then let everything else fall into its right place. . . .

Sharon Daugherty

Do not be anxious about anything, but in everything, by prayer and petition, with thanksgiving, present your requests to God. And the peace of God, which transcends all understanding, will guard your hearts and your minds in Christ Jesus.

Philippians 4:6,7 NIV

*D*oing the will of God is worth every test or trial you may face, because when you're trusting God, you will come out of each test or trial victorious.

Oretha Hagin

That the trial of your faith, being much more precious than of gold that perisheth, though it be tried with fire, might be found unto praise and honour and glory at the appearing of Jesus Christ.

1 Peter 1:7

25

*D*on't expect your husband to be to you that which only the Lord Jesus Himself can be.

Ruth Bell Graham

That which we have seen and heard declare we unto you, that ye also may have fellowship with us: and truly our fellowship is with the Father, and with his Son Jesus Christ.
1 John 1:3

would definitely say that it takes a lot of grace
— God's grace — . . . to be a Christian wife.

Betty Price

But by the grace of God I am what I am: and his grace which was bestowed upon me was not in vain; but I laboured more abundantly than they all: yet not I, but the grace of God which was with me.

1 Corinthians 15:10

27

*I*f you start your day with prayer and God's Word, you will have on the armor of God, your spirit will be filled with the Holy Spirit's fruits, and your heart will be sensitive to hear God's voice speaking to you.

Sharon Daugherty

And the disciples were filled with joy and with the Holy Spirit.

Acts 13:52 NIV

*I*f you want to move in authority in the Word, if you want to take the Word as authority over circumstances, you yourself must come under the authority of that Word. The Word has to be your total authority.

Marilyn Hickey

The centurion answered and said, Lord, I am not worthy that thou shouldest come under my roof: but speak the word only, and my servant shall be healed. For I am a man under authority, having soldiers under me: and I say to this man, Go, and he goeth; and to another, Come, and he cometh; and to my servant, Do this, and he doeth it.

Matthew 8:8,9

We are not to compare ourselves with others, but let Jesus be our example and learn to reflect the presence of God Who indwells us.

Joyce Meyer

For we dare not make ourselves of the number, or compare ourselves with some that commend themselves: but they measuring themselves by themselves, and comparing themselves among themselves, are not wise.

2 Corinthians 10:12

*G*od wants you to know who you are in Him so He can complete His work through you.

Cheryl Salem

Therefore if any man be in Christ, he is a new creature: old things are passed away; behold, all things are become new.

2 Corinthians 5:17

31

One wrong word can destroy a relationship. One right word can bond two lives together.

Brenda Timberlake

Pleasant words are as an honeycomb, sweet to the soul, and health to the bones.

Proverbs 16:24

*C*hoose to do what you can do, and God will help you do what you cannot do.

Joyce Meyer

And he said unto me, My grace is sufficient for thee: for my strength is made perfect in weakness. Most gladly therefore will I rather glory in my infirmities, that the power of Christ may rest upon me.

2 Corinthians 12:9

The Bible teaches us that we set the atmosphere in the home, and we do that by taking the Word of God and praying and confessing it for our home.

Marilyn Hickey

"His master replied, 'Well done, good and faithful servant! You have been faithful with a few things; I will put you in charge of many things. Come and share your master's happiness!'"

Matthew 25:21 NIV

*R*esist strife just as you would sin or sickness. Discord is deadly, and it is always of the devil. You can't afford it. It will paralyze the power of God in your life.

Gloria Copeland

May he strengthen your hearts so that you will be blameless and holy in the presence of our God and Father when our Lord Jesus comes with all his holy ones.

1 Thessalonians 3:13 NIV

*I*n the strength that comes from praising God, we can walk forth as an overcomer to do whatever is necessary.

Pat Harrison

I will go in the strength of the Lord God: I will make mention of thy righteousness, even of thine only.
Psalm 71:16

With Jesus inside us, we have the power to do what we could never do on our own.

Joyce Meyer

Jesus answered and said unto him, If a man love me, he will keep my words: and my Father will love him, and we will come unto him, and make our abode with him.

John 14:23

*I*t is He Who gives me the wisdom to plan my day, the intelligence to carry out each task and the energy to do it. And then He gives me the joy and satisfaction of achievement.

Marilyn Hickey

For the eyes of the Lord range throughout the earth to strengthen those whose hearts are fully committed to him.
2 Chronicles 16:9a NIV

*C*ontinue to look in the mirror of God's Word so that we will not forget that we are blessed in everything we do and all of our needs have already been met in Christ Jesus' glorious riches.

Jeri Williams

But the man who looks intently into the perfect law that gives freedom, and continues to do this, not forgetting what he has heard, but doing it — he will be blessed in what he does.

James 1:25 NIV

*O*ur Words and our mouths create the atmosphere that we're going to have in our home.

Brenda Timberlake

A man shall eat good by the fruit of his mouth: but the soul of the transgressors shall eat violence. He that keepeth his mouth keepeth his life: but he that openeth wide his lips shall have destruction.

Proverbs 13:2,3

*G*od is a miracle-working God, and there is nothing in your home that He cannot repair.

Marilyn Hickey

And Jesus looking upon them saith, With men it is impossible, but not with God: for with God all things are possible.

Mark 10:27

*I*f you are believing God for something, watch what comes out of your mouth. Keep on confessing the Word of God, and God will honor His Word.

Dodie Osteen

For with the heart man believeth unto righteousness; and with the mouth confession is made unto salvation.
Romans 10:10

As a woman, learn to release your faith; allow yourself to sincerely desire the good things which God has created in your world.

Daisy Osborn

For verily I say unto you, That whosoever shall say unto this mountain, Be thou removed, and be thou cast into the sea; and shall not doubt in his heart, but shall believe that those things which he saith shall come to pass; he shall have whatsoever he saith.

Mark 11:23

*Y*ou must depend solely on your relationship with the Lord to receive real happiness, peace and joy.

Bea Basansky

For the kingdom of God is not meat and drink; but righteousness, and peace, and joy in the Holy Ghost.
Romans 14:17

*I*t's important to let every fruit of righteousness become perfect unto full maturity within us.

Pat Harrison

I am the vine, ye are the branches: He that abideth in me, and I in him, the same bringeth forth much fruit: for without me ye can do nothing.

John 15:5

As contemporary women in the glitz of dazzling feministic expectations, we must rest confidently in who and what the Word of God says about us.

Jeri Williams

Only let your conversation be as it becometh the gospel of Christ: that whether I come and see you, or else be absent, I may hear of your affairs, that ye stand fast in one spirit, with one mind striving together for the faith of the gospel.
Philippians 1:27

The one essential thing is to enter into a love relationship with God in which we worship Him and focus on His will for our lives.

Mary Jean Pidgeon

And be not conformed to this world: but be ye transformed by the renewing of your mind, that ye may prove what is that good, and acceptable, and perfect, will of God.

Romans 12:2

By always feeding upon Jesus, the Word, we dwell and continue in our perfection in Him.

Pat Harrison

And God raised us up with Christ and seated us with him in the heavenly realms in Christ Jesus.
Ephesians 2:6 NIV

*F*ill your house with the Word, and the house will fill up with riches and wealth.

Marilyn Hickey

And by knowledge shall the chambers be filled with all precious and pleasant riches.

Proverbs 24:4

*Y*our natural ability does not determine your usefulness. All you have to be is one who lives in the presence of God. He has the ability!

Gloria Copeland

For ye see your calling, brethren, how that not many wise men after the flesh, not many mighty, not many noble, are called.

1 Corinthians 1:26

*Y*ou may make some mistakes, but if your heart is daily yielded to God and you make the effort to let His kingdom rule in your life, God will "make up the difference."

Sharon Daugherty

And he said unto me, My grace is sufficient for thee: for my strength is made perfect in weakness. Most gladly therefore will I rather glory in my infirmities, that the power of Christ may rest upon me. Therefore I take pleasure in infirmities, in reproaches, in necessities, in persecutions, in distresses for Christ's sake: for when I am weak, then am I strong.

2 Corinthians 12:9,10

The real Proverbs 31 woman knows that it takes more than makeup to be beautiful . . . it takes Jesus!

Cheryl Salem

Whose adorning let it not be that outward adorning of plaiting the hair, and of wearing of gold, or of putting on of apparel; But let it be the hidden man of the heart, in that which is not corruptible, even the ornament of a meek and quiet spirit, which is in the sight of God of great price.

1 Peter 3:3,4

A virtuous woman trusts Jesus completely because she knows Him. And she knows Him because she has spent time with Him.

Janice Subers

This is the confidence we have in approaching God: that if we ask anything according to his will, he hears us. And if we know that he hears us — whatever we ask — we know that we have what we asked of him.

1 John 5:14,15 NIV

As a wife, mother and woman, you need to plant seeds of love, praise, truth, confidence, admiration and so forth in your home.

Bea Basansky

Be not deceived; God is not mocked: for whatsoever a man soweth, that shall he also reap.

Galatians 6:7

When you enter into God's new covenant,
many promises become yours . . . promises not only
for you, but also for your mate and for your children.

Marilyn Hickey

But now hath he obtained a more excellent ministry, by
how much also he is the mediator of a better covenant,
which was established upon better promises.
Hebrews 8:6

When God is directing your course, you can't go wrong in life.

Oretha Hagin

For as many as are led by the Spirit of God, they are the sons of God.

Romans 8:14

$\mathcal{W}$e must develop to the fullest knowledge of love, because by this God's glory is manifested and recognized.

Pat Harrison

And we have known and believed the love that God hath to us. God is love; and he that dwelleth in love dwelleth in God, and God in him.

1 John 4:16

*Y*ou must become faithful and diligent to spend the time it takes to get to know God. Set apart time everyday to fellowship with Him and get to know Him personally.

Gloria Copeland

And this is life eternal, that they might know thee the only true God, and Jesus Christ, whom thou hast sent.
John 17:3

*C*ommit yourself to do the will of God and spend time with Him by praying in the Spirit and in the understanding, and by studying the Word.

Betty Price

What is it then? I will pray with the spirit, and I will pray with the understanding also: I will sing with the spirit, and I will sing with the understanding also.
1 Corinthians 14:15

*G*od is at work in you as a woman, reaching people through your hands, through your love, through your life.

Daisy Osborn

For it is God which worketh in you both to will and to do of his good pleasure.

Philippians 2:13

*B*eing a woman of God provides the greatest satisfaction and fulfillment a woman could ever desire.

Beverly LaHaye

Favour is deceitful, and beauty is vain: but a woman that feareth the Lord, she shall be praised.
Proverbs 31:30

*I*f you want to have a happy marriage, become your mate's best friend. Listen to one another. Nurture and care for each other.

Brenda Timberlake

Submitting yourselves one to another in the fear of God.
Ephesians 5:21

Your family . . . is not only one of your most precious gifts, when it's operating in harmony, it's one of your most powerful resources.

Gloria Copeland

For our struggle is not against flesh and blood, but against the rulers, against the authorities, against the powers of this dark world and against the spiritual forces of evil in the heavenly realms.

Ephesians 6:12 NIV

As a wife sows patience with her husband's efforts to be a better friend, she will reap more patience from Him.

Brenda Timberlake

But this I say, He which soweth sparingly shall reap also sparingly; and he which soweth bountifully shall reap also bountifully.

2 Corinthians 9:6

Trust and faith bring joy to life and help relationships grow to their maximum potential.

Joyce Meyer

Now the God of hope fill you with all joy and peace in believing, that ye may abound in hope, through the power of the Holy Ghost.

Romans 15:13

There is only one way you can tell if you are a leader . . . look behind to see if anyone is following!

Margaret Hicks

Let no man despise thy youth; but be thou an example of the believers, in word, in conversation, in charity, in spirit, in faith, in purity.

1 Timothy 4:12

*G*od has given each one of us our own unique talents in areas where we can really excel and let our lights shine.

Lindsay Roberts

Let your light so shine before men, that they may see your good works, and glorify your Father which is in heaven.

Matthew 5:16

The reason we're here is to let God's love flow out of us.

Pat Harrison

And walk in love, as Christ also hath loved us, and hath given himself for us an offering and a sacrifice to God for a sweet-smelling savour.

Ephesians 5:2

*T*here is a wonderful reward for a peaceful, loving home.

Margaret Hicks

A Song of degrees. Blessed is every one that feareth the Lord; that walketh in his ways. For thou shalt eat the labour of thine hands: happy shalt thou be, and it shall be well with thee.

Psalm 128:1,2

Stop looking at your family from your own perspective and start seeing it as God sees it — as a powerhouse.

Gloria Copeland

Now if we are children, then we are heirs — heirs of God and co-heirs with Christ, if indeed we share in his sufferings in order that we may also share in his glory.
Romans 8:17 NIV

*G*od has good things for you and your family. They are all part of His covenant with you as His child.

Marilyn Hickey

Know therefore that the Lord thy God, he is God, the faithful God, which keepeth covenant and mercy with them that love him and keep his commandments to a thousand generations.

Deuteronomy 7:9

*W*hen a woman is secure in the Lord Jesus, when she knows that she is covered by His blood, then she has no need of being fearful.

Dodie Osteen

For you granted him authority over all people that he might give eternal life to all those you have given him. Now this is eternal life: that they may know you, the only true God, and Jesus Christ, whom you have sent.

John 17:2,3 NIV

*G*od never fails. And no matter how difficult the test or trial, faithfulness always reaps the reward.

Oretha Hagin

That ye be not slothful, but followers of them who through faith and patience inherit the promises.
Hebrews 6:12

We are not walking in the Word if our thoughts are opposite of what it says. We are not walking in the Word if we are not thinking in the Word.

Joyce Meyer

If ye then be risen with Christ, seek those things which are above, where Christ sitteth on the right hand of God. Set your affection on things above, not on things on the earth.
Colossians 3:1,2

*A*s a believer, the potential for excellence is within us. God has given us the key, the Bible, to unlock our treasure chest and expose His glorious nature to those around us.

Janice Subers

Do not let this Book of the Law depart from your mouth; meditate on it day and night, so that you may be careful to do everything written in it. Then you will be prosperous and successful.

Joshua 1:8 NIV

We set the atmosphere in the home, and we do that by taking the Word of God and praying and confessing it for our home.

Marilyn Hickey

Through faith we understand that the worlds were framed by the word of God, so that things which are seen were not made of things which do appear.

Hebrews 11:3

$\mathcal{W}$e must remember that all the words we speak
have the potential to produce life or death.

Bea Basansky

*Death and life are in the power of the tongue: and they
that love it shall eat the fruit thereof.*
Proverbs 18:21

We do not need self-confidence; we need God-confidence!

Joyce Meyer

For we are the circumcision, which worship God in the spirit, and rejoice in Christ Jesus, and have no confidence in the flesh.

Philippians 3:3

*G*od will use you if you make yourself available to Him.

Carolyn Savelle

And I thank Christ Jesus our Lord, who hath enabled me, for that he counted me faithful, putting me into the ministry.

1 Timothy 1:12

*I*f you will purpose to keep the Word given to you, the Devil cannot snatch it away.

Brenda Timberlake

Therefore we ought to give the more earnest heed to the things which we have heard, lest at any time we should let them slip.

Hebrews 2:1

*H*ours of prayer and study is of no effect if you do not enforce what is learned.

Cathy Duplantis

Therefore whosoever heareth these sayings of mine, and doeth them, I will liken him unto a wise man, which built his house upon a rock.

Matthew 7:24

Our heart is the earpiece with which we hear the voice of the Holy Spirit. We must guard the affections of our heart with all diligence so that it does not become hardened and dull of hearing.

Jeri Williams

So, as the Holy Spirit says: "Today, if you hear his voice, do not harden your hearts as you did in the rebellion, during the time of testing in the desert."

Hebrews 3:7,8 NIV

$\mathcal{L}$ove is not conditional on your emotions. You do not love a person because they are sweet to you. Love, in the Bible, is an act of faith. When you act in faith, you will notice that your emotions begin to go with it.

Marilyn Hickey

Bear with each other and forgive whatever grievances you may have against one another. Forgive as the Lord forgave you. And over all these virtues put on love, which binds them all together in perfect unity.
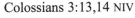
Colossians 3:13,14 NIV

*Y*our attitude toward others is a reflection of your attitude toward yourself.

Daisy Osborn

So ought men to love their wives as their own bodies. He that loveth his wife loveth himself.

Ephesians 5:28

The virtuous woman is careful to see that her family has the things they need.

Pat Harrison

She looketh well to the ways of her household, and eateth not the bread of idleness.

Proverbs 31:27

*I*t doesn't matter where you are or what you have, but what you do with where you are and what you have.

Mary Jean Pidgeon

This is a faithful saying, and these things I will that thou affirm constantly, that they which have believed in God might be careful to maintain good works. These things are good and profitable unto men.

Titus 3:8

*B*eing a doer of the Word is not always a physical act, but often an attitude of the heart.

Jeri Williams

But be ye doers of the word, and not hearers only, deceiving your own selves.

James 1:22

Once the Holy Spirit has revealed an area in your life that must be crucified, it is your responsibility to eliminate it from your life.

Cathy Duplantis

And they that are Christ's have crucified the flesh with the affections and lusts.

Galatians 5:24

Women were created to be winners with God.
Failure is never His will . . . insecurity and uncertainty
are not God's plan for you as a woman believer.

Daisy Osborn

*Then you will have success if you are careful to
observe the decrees and laws that the Lord gave Moses
for Israel. Be strong and courageous. Do not be afraid
or discouraged.*

1 Chronicles 22:13 NIV

89

When we believe His Word for our lives, He will perform it in our lives.

Sharon Daugherty

For the scripture saith, Whosoever believeth on him shall not be ashamed. For there is no difference between the Jew and the Greek: for the same Lord over all is rich unto all that call upon him.

Romans 10:11,12

90

*T*ake time to get away from the world and study God's Word. Meditate on it and let it change you from the inside out.

Gloria Copeland

But we all, with open face beholding as in a glass the glory of the Lord, are changed into the same image from glory to glory, even as by the Spirit of the Lord.
2 Corinthians 3:18

*T*here is no greater honor or privilege than that of being a blessing to someone in need.

Carolyn Savelle

Withhold not good from them to whom it is due, when it is in the power of thine hand to do it.

Proverbs 3:27

*T*here is nothing more rewarding in life than to fulfill God's perfect will and to be a blessing to others.

Oretha Hagin

And be not conformed to this world: but be ye transformed by the renewing of your mind, that ye may prove what is that good, and acceptable, and perfect, will of God.

Romans 12:2

*G*od's love for you is perfect . . . and unconditional.
When you fail, He keeps on loving you because His
love is not based on you, but on Him.

Joyce Meyer

But God, who is rich in mercy, for his great love wherewith
he loved us, Even when we were dead in sins, hath
quickened us together with Christ, by grace ye are saved.
Ephesians 2:4,5

*G*od is concerned about your total existence . . . spiritual, emotional and physical. He wants all of your life to be fulfilling and delightful.

Marilyn Hickey

For I rejoiced greatly, when the brethren came and testified of the truth that is in thee, even as thou walkest in the truth.

3 John 3

*I*f you want to see people's lives touched and changed by the Lord, you must love them.

Oretha Hagin

For, brethren, ye have been called unto liberty; only use not liberty for an occasion to the flesh, but by love serve one another.

Galatians 5:13

*A*lways see through the eyes of love, hear through the ears of love, and do the action of love.

Pat Harrison

A new commandment I give unto you, That ye love one another; as I have loved you, that ye also love one another. By this shall all men know that ye are my disciples, if ye have love one to another.

John 13:34,35

*T*he Bible does not tell us to run here and there to fulfill ourselves spiritually. The Word says we must continue to do what we know to do, but that does not come at the expense of our families.

Pat Harrison

That they may teach the young women to be sober, to love their husbands, to love their children, To be discreet, chaste, keepers at home, good, obedient to their own husbands, that the word of God be not blasphemed.

Titus 2:4,5

God is so gracious to His children and is concerned about every area of our lives, including the intimacy that exists between husband and wife.

Betty Price

Trust in the Lord with all thine heart; and lean not unto thine own understanding. In all thy ways acknowledge him, and he shall direct thy paths.
Proverbs 3:5,6

*A*n honest daily examination of your spirit is essential to growing good fruit.

Cathy Duplantis

Every branch in me that beareth not fruit he taketh away: and every branch that beareth fruit, he purgeth it, that it may bring forth more fruit.

John 15:2

The only way to find God's direction for your life daily is by starting your day with Him.

Sharon Daugherty

O God, thou art my God; early will I seek thee: my soul thirsteth for thee, my flesh longeth for thee in a dry and thirsty land, where no water is.

Psalm 63:1

*W*hen you're doing what God has told you to do and you're serving Him, it doesn't matter how tough the going gets; God is always faithful.

Oretha Hagin

Let us hold fast the profession of our faith without wavering; for he is faithful that promised.
Hebrews 10:23

$\mathscr{P}$ut your confidence in the Lord Jesus Christ and His Word no matter what happens. He is your hope. God will surely reward your trust in Him.

Dodie Osteen

Cast not away therefore your confidence, which hath great recompence of reward. For ye have need of patience, that, after ye have done the will of God, ye might receive the promise.

Hebrews 10:35,36

*Y*ou must continually put the Word in your mind to keep it in agreement and at peace with your spirit.

Pat Harrison

Finally, brethren, whatsoever things are true, whatsoever things are honest, whatsoever things are just, whatsoever things are pure, whatsoever things are lovely, whatsoever things are of good report; if there be any virtue, and if there be any praise, think on these things.

Philippians 4:8

*G*ive God's Word first place in your heart
because it is life and health to your body.

Dodie Osteen

*My son, attend to my words; incline thine ear unto my
sayings. Let them not depart from thine eyes; keep
them in the midst of thine heart. For they are life unto
those that find them, and health to all their flesh.*

Proverbs 4:20-22

Commit and submit your talents, dreams, and desires to God. Let Him sanctify you, then seize those opportunities He makes available to you.

Nancy Cole

So we say with confidence, "The Lord is my helper; I will not be afraid. What can man do to me?"

Hebrews 13:6 NIV

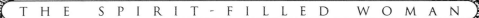
*D*on't disdain the talents that God has given to you. . . . look for ways and opportunities in which to use your God-given talents . . . whatever they are.

Lindsay Roberts

Do not neglect your gift, which was given you through a prophetic message when the body of elders laid their hands on you. Be diligent in these matters; give yourself wholly to them, so that everyone may see your progress.

1 Timothy 4:14,15 NIV

*P*leasing the Lord takes two things: obedience and willingness.

Cheryl Salem

If ye be willing and obedient, ye shall eat the good of the land.

Isaiah 1:19

There is nothing more fulfilling in life than to do what God has called you to do.

Oretha Hagin

Moreover whom he did predestinate, them he also called: and whom he called, them he also justified: and whom he justified, them he also glorified. What shall we then say to these things? If God be for us, who can be against us?

Romans 8:30,31

very woman has a divine call. For some the call is diversified and can change along life's journey. But each stage is preparation for the next.

Freda Lindsay

But now hath God set the members every one of them in the body, as it hath pleased him.

1 Corinthians 12:18

*Y*ou were born both to be a blessing and to be blessed. But most of all, you were born to desire God above everything else.

Carolyn Savelle

As the hart panteth after the water brooks, so panteth my soul after thee, O God. My soul thirsteth for God, for the living God: when shall I come and appear before God?

Psalm 42:1,2

*M*ake your faith effectual by acknowledging every good thing that God has in your household.

Marilyn Hickey

And my God will meet all your needs according to his glorious riches in Christ Jesus.

Philippians 4:19 NIV

*G*od will honor your faith in doing your part to bring divine order into your home.

Bea Basansky

She watches over the affairs of her household and does not eat the bread of idleness. Her children arise and call her blessed; her husband also, and he praises her.
Proverbs 31:27,28 NIV

*Y*ou need to train yourself to be sensitive to the Holy Spirit throughout the day so you can minister Christ's life to those He may bring in contact with you.

Bea Basansky

And be not drunk with wine, wherein is excess; but be filled with the Spirit; Speaking to yourselves in psalms and hymns and spiritual songs, singing and making melody in your heart to the Lord.

Ephesians 5:18,19

114

*I*f we are submitted to Jesus and He is Lord of our life, we should not wonder what He can do for us, but we should ask, "What can we do for Him?"

Pat Harrison

Carry each other's burdens, and in this way you will fulfill the law of Christ.

Galatians 6:2 NIV

*L*earn to be sensitive to what the Spirit of God tells you, rather than what your five senses dictate.

Carolyn Savelle

For as many as are led by the Spirit of God, they are the sons of God.

Romans 8:14

*G*od's will for every area of our lives is "Growth."

Sharon Daugherty

But speaking the truth in love, may grow up into him in all things, which is the head, even Christ.
Ephesians 4:15

*L*ife is just so much sweeter when you're walking closely with the Lord, loving Him and doing what He wants you to do.

Oretha Hagin

God is faithful, by whom ye were called unto the fellowship of his Son Jesus Christ our Lord.

1 Corinthians 1:9

*T*here is only one way that you can accomplish the will of God in your life . . . obeying His Spirit one day at a time.

Gloria Copeland

Wherefore be ye not unwise, but understanding what the will of the Lord is. And be not drunk with wine, wherein is excess; but be filled with the Spirit.
Ephesians 5:17,18

A woman of God will never be separated from the flow of God's power and ability in her life. Her life comes from within.

Margaret Hicks

For ye are dead, and your life is hid with Christ in God. When Christ, who is our life, shall appear, then shall ye also appear with him in glory.

Colossians 3:3,4

As a woman with real life in you, you liberate your God-given talents, your gifts, your power of choice to reach out to serve, to bless, to heal and to lift your world.

Daisy Osborn

The thief cometh not, but for to steal, and to kill, and to destroy: I am come that they might have life, and that they might have it more abundantly.

John 10:10

*J*t is important for you to come to grips with the fact that your life will not get straightened out until your mind does.

Joyce Meyer

Casting down imaginations, and every high thing that exalteth itself against the knowledge of God, and bringing into captivity every thought to the obedience of Christ.
2 Corinthians 10:5

To successfully have the outward appearance of radiance, vibrancy and happiness, we must also have inner peace.

Bea Basansky

And let the peace of God rule in your hearts, to the which also ye are called in one body; and be ye thankful.

Colossians 3:15

123

*I*f we will keep our eyes on what is right and make sure that our motives line up with God's Word, right will always win in the end.

Betty Price

And said, If thou wilt diligently hearken to the voice of the Lord thy God, and wilt do that which is right in his sight, and wilt give ear to his commandments, and keep all his statutes, I will put none of these diseases upon thee, which I have brought upon the Egyptians: for I am the Lord that healeth thee.

Exodus 15:26

*N*o amount of human love, beauty, wealth or accomplishments can substitute for the value and preciousness that obedience to the Word of God imparts.

Jeri Williams

Thou shalt keep therefore his statutes, and his commandments, which I command thee this day, that it may go well with thee, and with thy children after thee, and that thou mayest prolong thy days upon the earth, which the Lord thy God giveth thee, for ever.

Deuteronomy 4:40

*G*od is a loving Father Who wants His children well and happy.

Dodie Osteen

If ye then, being evil, know how to give good gifts unto your children, how much more shall your Father which is in heaven give good things to them that ask him?

Matthew 7:11

*G*od wants you to be free to be yourself while you are seeking to be like Him.

Sharon Daugherty

For whom he did foreknow, he also did predestinate to be conformed to the image of his Son, that he might be the firstborn among many brethren.

Romans 8:29

*Y*ou must pray on a daily basis. . . . That is part of keeping your home in order — full of joy, peace, love and understanding.

Pat Harrison

Pray without ceasing.

1 Thessalonians 5:17

When we live in peace instead of strife, we are enjoying one of God's most powerful blessings — a love-ruled home.

Gloria Copeland

"Come to me, all you who are weary and burdened, and I will give you rest."

Matthew 11:29 NIV

*W*hatever your need is, find the promise you need in the Word of God, then ask according to His Word. God's will is His Word.

Dodie Osteen

If ye abide in me, and my words abide in you, ye shall ask what ye will, and it shall be done unto you.

John 15:7

*T*he more time a person spends meditating on the Word, the more he (she) will reap from the Word.

Joyce Meyer

O how love I thy law! it is my meditation all the day. Thou through thy commandments hast made me wiser than mine enemies: for they are ever with me. I have more understanding than all my teachers: for thy testimonies are my meditation.

Psalm 119:97-99

When you begin to take care of the needs of others, God will make certain that all your needs are met.

Carolyn Savelle

He that giveth unto the poor shall not lack: but he that hideth his eyes shall have many a curse.

Proverbs 28:27

*C*hoose to give of yourself, of your time, of your abilities and of your talents to make the world around you better.

Daisy Osborn

Heal the sick, cleanse the lepers, raise the dead, cast out devils: freely ye have received, freely give.
Matthew 10:8

*W*oman was created perfect . . . and . . . through spiritual adoption in Jesus Christ, we can again be the perfect woman God created us to be.

Pat Harrison

Neither was man created for woman, but woman for man.
1 Corinthians 11:9 NIV

eject any voice or any influence that would demean you or categorize you as mediocre or as an ordinary human person. You are unique.

Daisy Osborn

And when he putteth forth his own sheep, he goeth before them, and the sheep follow him: for they know his voice. And a stranger will they not follow, but will flee from him: for they know not the voice of strangers.

John 10:4,5

*A*s women of God, we are led toward success through the wisdom He gives us.

Mary Jean Pidgeon

He layeth up sound wisdom for the righteous: he is a buckler to them that walk uprightly.
Proverbs 2:7

*G*od's Spirit and His Word can change our lives into women of grace and wisdom.

Sharon Daugherty

But we all, with open face beholding as in a glass the glory of the Lord, are changed into the same image from glory to glory, even as by the Spirit of the Lord.
2 Corinthians 3:18

*L*earn to see yourself as God sees you . . . saved, filled with the Spirit, healed, prosperous and blessed.

Cheryl Salem

For in him dwelleth all the fulness of the Godhead bodily.
And ye are complete in him, which is the head of all
principality and power.

Colossians 2:9,10

We can be beautiful . . . when we allow our beauty to come out of our regenerated spirit, by the Holy Spirit.

Bea Basansky

Whose adorning let it not be that outward adorning of plaiting the hair, and of wearing of gold, or of putting on of apparel; But let it be the hidden man of the heart, in that which is not corruptible, even the ornament of a meek and quiet spirit, which is in the sight of God of great price.

1 Peter 3:3,4

*B*e the woman God intends you to be by your manner of living.

Pat Harrison

For the eyes of the Lord are over the righteous, and his ears are open unto their prayers: but the face of the Lord is against them that do evil.

1 Peter 3:12

God created woman in His own image, the same as He did man.

Daisy Osborn

So God created man in his own image, in the image of God created he him; male and female created he them.
Genesis 1:27

*C*hristian women have a very special birth-right. They are divine citizens with a divine heritage and birth-right.

Marilyn Hickey

But we are citizens of the state (commonwealth, homeland) which is in heaven, and from it also we earnestly and patiently await [the coming of] the Lord Jesus Christ (the Messiah) [as] Savior.

Philippians 3:20 AMP

*H*ave the courage to individualize yourself . . .
to be and to stay unique.

Daisy Osborn

*I can do all things through Christ which strengtheneth
me.*

Philippians 4:13

143

As "A New Creation" you don't have to allow the old things that happened to you to keep affecting your new life in Christ.

Joyce Meyer

But God forbid that I should glory, save in the cross of our Lord Jesus Christ, by whom the world is crucified unto me, and I unto the world. For in Christ Jesus neither circumcision availeth any thing, nor uncircumcision, but a new creature.

Galatians 6:14,15

I have found that the more we are identified with Christ, the more freedom we have from the pressures of other people's images of us.

Nancy Cole

Then Jesus came to them and said, "Authority in heaven and on earth has been given to me."
Matthew 28:18 NIV

Wife and motherhood duties fall into order as we first submit our ways to God.

Sharon Daugherty

Come, let us bow down in worship, let us kneel before the Lord our Maker.

Psalm 95:6 NIV

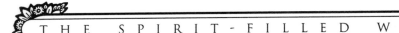

*G*od made you unique and special and gave you a high calling to be a wife and mother.

Evelyn Roberts

And the Lord God caused a deep sleep to fall upon Adam, and he slept: and he took one of his ribs, and closed up the flesh instead thereof; And the rib, which the Lord God had taken from man, made he a woman, and brought her unto the man. And Adam said, This is now bone of my bones, and flesh of my flesh: she shall be called Woman, because she was taken out of Man.

Genesis 2:21-23

The Word is not just paper and ink. . . . It's life.

Pat Harrison

It is the spirit that quickeneth; the flesh profiteth nothing: the words that I speak unto you, they are spirit, and they are life.

John 6:63

*G*od is looking for women who dare to believe His Word!

Mary Jean Pidgeon

And Jesus answering saith unto them, Have faith in God.

Mark 11:22

We must be obedient to do whatever He tells us to do, no matter how insignificant it may seem.

Carolyn Savelle

But be ye doers of the word, and not hearers only, deceiving your own selves.

James 1:22

*I*f you obey God in the small things, the rewards will be great.

Oretha Hagin

His lord said unto him, Well done, good and faithful servant; thou hast been faithful over a few things, I will make thee ruler over many things: enter thou into the joy of thy lord.

Matthew 25:23

As daughters of God, we are no longer our own. As we learn how to love the Father God, it causes us to know what to say, what to do for our intimate friend — our mate-on-earth.

Brenda Timberlake

Beloved, let us love one another: for love is of God; and every one that loveth is born of God, and knoweth God. He that loveth not knoweth not God; for God is love.
1 John 4:7,8

*Y*ou are skillfully and carefully handcrafted to be suitable, adaptable, and completing to a man. The way you become those things is by continually surrounding the one God has given you with aid and assistance.

Pat Harrison

How long will you wander, O unfaithful daughter? The Lord will create a new thing on earth — a woman will surround a man.

Jeremiah 31:22 NIV

*R*adiance comes naturally to the one who is at peace with herself and God.

Cheryl Salem

Therefore being justified by faith, we have peace with God through our Lord Jesus Christ.

Romans 5:1

*I*t is absolutely impossible to worry and live in peace at the same time.

Joyce Meyer

Be careful for nothing; but in every thing by prayer and supplication with thanksgiving let your requests be made known unto God. And the peace of God, which passeth all understanding, shall keep your hearts and minds through Christ Jesus.

Philippians 4:6,7

True womanhood can never be measured by a man's affections or society's praises, but by a woman's own character as measured by the Word of God.

Nancy Cole

"Do not grieve, for the joy of the Lord is your strength."
Nehemiah 8:10b NIV

*I*t's not your conversation or manner of living in the natural realm that counts, but your manner of living according to Jesus Christ as Lord of your life.

Pat Harrison

Only let your conversation be as it becometh the gospel of Christ: that whether I come and see you, or else be absent, I may hear of your affairs, that ye stand fast in one spirit, with one mind striving together for the faith of the gospel.

Philippians 1:27

*B*y doing what the Lord tells you to do, blessings will come to you in abundance.

Pat Harrison

Keep therefore the words of this covenant, and do them, that ye may prosper in all that ye do.

Deuteronomy 29:9

*I*t is just beautiful what God can do for you if you stay faithful to what He has called you to do.

Oretha Hagin

If ye be willing and obedient, ye shall eat the good of the land.

Isaiah 1:19